NATIVE WOMEN OF COURAGE

Kelly Fournel

7th
GENERATION

Summertown, Tennessee

Library of Congress Cataloging-in-Publication Data

Fournel, Kelly, 1976-
    Native women of courage / by Kelly Fournel.
        p. cm.
    ISBN 978-0-9779183-2-4
    1. Indian women—Biography—Juvenile literature. I. Title.

    E98.W8F68 2007
    305.48'897—dc22
    [B]   2007028538

Published in the United States by
7th Generation
P.O. Box 99
Summertown, TN 38483
888-260-8458
www.bookpubco.com

Printed in the U.S.

ISBN 978-0-9779183-2-4

Photo credits found on page 83.

Seventh Generation is committed to preserving ancient forests and natural resources. We have elected to print this title on paper which is 100%
postconsumer recycled and processed chlorine free. As a result of our
paper choice, we have saved the following natural resources:

    21 trees
    1,834 lbs. CO2 equivalent
    7,613 gallons waste water
    978 pounds solid waste
    15 million BTUs total energy

(Paper calculations from Environmental Defense www.papercalculator.org)

We are a member of Green Press Initiative.
For more information about Green Press Initiative visit:
www.greenpressinitive.org

For my mother,
who lives life with integrity,
passion, and humor.

CONTENTS

The women featured in this book are role models because they have all worked hard at creating opportunities for themselves despite facing different challenges. Women of all ages and cultural backgrounds experience discrimination (unfair treatment based on prejudice), but through hard work, dedication, love, and self-respect, these featured women—and others like them around the world—have risen above this unfavorable treatment and have made a positive difference to their communities.

It wasn't an easy job figuring out which great women to include in this book. Both Canada and the United States are filled with examples of women of all backgrounds who live their lives the best way they can and should be celebrated. By featuring women of First Nations backgrounds, I hope to bring attention to a minority group that is still largely ignored by our greater society and needs to be applauded for their achievements, sacrifices, and passions.

Although it is impossible to feature an example from every region and every Native culture that exists, I have tried to give a balanced look at women from history and modern times, from Canada and the

United States, who have different skills and achievements. It is my hope that they will inspire you to become more aware of the potential that lies inside of each of us, regardless of where we live and which culture we call our own.

Kelly Fournel is a Métis author who was born in Winnipeg, Manitoba, and raised in Calgary, Alberta. She obtained a B.Sc. in archaeology from the University of Calgary and a graduate diploma in book and magazine publishing from Centennial College in Toronto, Ontario. She and her husband live with their fat cat in Prince Albert, Saskatchewan.

Kelly Fournel

Suzanne Rochon-Burnett

Suzanne Rochon-Burnett—affectionately called Suzy by her family and friends—was born in St. Adèle, Québec, on March 10, 1935. The tiny girl spent the first six months of her life in a Montréal hospital battling health problems. Suzy grew up on a family farm in the Laurentian Mountains, where she learned from her family that having a generous spirit was just as important as being able to work hard.

From an early age, Suzy witnessed what it was like to run a small business. Her father, Acheille, was a mechanic with his own garage. Her mother, Jeanne, brought extra money into

Suzanne Rochon-Burnett

the home by producing knitted goods. At the age of seven, Suzy became the courier for her mother's business. It was Suzy's responsibility to drop off wool to local women who would knit her mother's designs, then pick up the various knitted pieces and bring them home, where they were assembled into sweaters. The finished items would later be sold to tourists at local ski hills.

Suzy was a Métis—a person who is a part of a distinct culture that was created out of the unions of First Nations people with French or British settlers who had come to Canada. Before Suzy left home to start school, her parents told her to not talk about her First Nations heritage with the teachers or the other students. They were afraid that when their daughter left the protection of their loving home, she would face the racism and prejudice that were regularly experienced by First Nations people. Her parents only wanted to protect her from discrimination, but their instructions left Suzy wondering what was wrong with being Aboriginal.

The nuns at the school were strict teachers who demanded good behavior and attention to one's lessons. Children who didn't comply were often disciplined with a rap across the knuckles, and Suzy's knuckles endured their fair share of "discipline." She said it was the treatment she received at school that caused her to develop a rebellious streak. Nonetheless, by the time she had finished school, the high standards of the nuns had resulted in Suzy's trademark ability to speak flawless French.

These hard-earned, impeccable speaking skills would prove to be beneficial soon enough.

After graduating from high school, Suzy attended the local business college in St. Jerome. She studied English, shorthand (a method of writing quickly by using abbreviations or symbols for words or phrases), and typing. Because her generation was brought up to believe that if women chose to work outside the home, they were limited to jobs such as nursing, teaching, or secretarial work, Suzy set her sights on finding employment as a secretary. Her first job interview was with the owner of the local mill, and Suzy was quite excited about the possibility of working so close to home. Her hopes were dashed when the mill owner rejected her for the job. He felt that Suzy had too much potential to work in such a small town.

Suzy tried to keep her spirits up and soon heard that St. Jerome was going to have a new radio station. In the 1950s, broadcast journalism was heavily dominated by men, but Suzy was not intimidated by being in the minority. If anything, the discrimination she had faced at school, combined with strong support from her family, strengthened her belief that she could accomplish whatever she set her mind to. Suzy not only got an on-air job at the station, but by the age of twenty she also was writing regular newspaper columns, hosting two radio shows, and managing public relations for the station.

Suzy's years at school with the strict nuns had finally paid off. Her ability to speak French clearly and flawlessly helped her distinguish herself during the early years of her radio career. Her professional reputation was growing, but because she was determined to keep on challenging herself, she took public relations and marketing classes at McGill University in Montréal. This was a huge accomplishment for anybody, but especially so for a young Métis woman living at a time when society heavily favored the career advancements of men over their female counterparts.

With the growing success of her career in journalism, Suzy started traveling to Paris and Montréal to cover newsworthy events for different radio stations. Travel allowed her the opportunity to meet other successful women working in journalism, and these new female acquaintances were generous with their advice and support. Suzy started to branch out; she balanced working in broadcasting with modeling. One of her modeling jobs took her to New York City, where she appeared in television commercials.

As Suzy's confidence grew, so did her desire to own her own business. By the early 1960s, she decided to do something entirely different. She combined her interest in art with her desire to be her own boss and purchased an old lodge in the Laurentian Mountains. She renovated the lodge and turned it into an upscale inn and art gallery; her new business was a huge success.

One day, a friend talked Suzy into standing in for her on a date with a man from Ontario. His name was Gordon Burnett, and he owned a radio station in Niagara Falls. After getting past some initial awkwardness and misunderstanding, because Suzy's English was not all that good yet, Suzy and Gordon quickly became an item. When they married, she sold her inn and the couple moved to St. Catharines, Ontario. After the birth of their daughter, Michele-Elise, Suzy stayed at home until it was time for Michele-Elise to start school. Then she decided it was time to return to broadcasting.

Suzy produced a French-language show called *Chanson à la Française* from a small studio in her home. This one-hour show, which focused on French artists, was so popular with listeners that it soon grew to two hours, and eventually to a four-hour show. The Ontario Ministry of Culture was so impressed with Suzy's show that they sponsored and distributed the program to radio stations across Ontario. With so many new listeners throughout the province and an established listener base in Quebec, Suzy was offered the chance to be the Canadian Broadcasting Corporation's knowledgeable authority on all things dealing with French culture for their prestigious daily show *Morningside*.

By the mid-1980s, Suzy had channeled her passion for the arts and for raising awareness of First Nations' issues into the creation of a company that would promote Aboriginal artists and their concerns. This new company, Kakekalanicks Inc., would serve as a consulting firm for various media outlets, with the aim of educating people about the continued exploitation of Aboriginal people and their art. Suzy also brought awareness of Aboriginal issues to the television industry. When she volunteered as a board member for TVOntario, the province's educational public television broadcaster, Suzy introduced a new policy that would help journalists work with First Nations people of Ontario and allow Aboriginal representation on the station's Advisory Councils.

In 1995, Suzy purchased a country music radio station in Welland, Ontario, and became the first Aboriginal person in Canada to own a private, commercial radio station.

Despite her busy life, Suzy always found time to give back to her community by volunteering with various organizations, such as TVOntario, the Canadian Council for Aboriginal Business, the Ontario Arts Council, and the Canadian Native Arts Foundation. For her years of helping others within and outside of First Nations communities, she received many awards, including an honorary degree from Brock University, the Eagle Feather (Canada's highest First Nations honor), the Governor General Confederacy Medal, the Order of Ontario, and the Order of Canada (Canada's highest honor). Perhaps Suzy achieved so much because of her motto: "You have to keep trying. . . . Even if you fall flat on your face, you're still moving forward."

In 2004, Suzy left the broadcasting field to focus on her health. She had developed an incurable lung disease, but true to form, she wasn't going to give up without a fight. In February 2006, Suzy became the first woman to be inducted into the Canadian Council for Aboriginal Business Hall of Fame. Her acceptance speech focused on the pride she felt in being a part of such a grand community of people, the love she felt for her family, and the fun she'd had over the years. Despite her obvious challenges with breathing, Suzy conveyed to her audience that she was still a woman of strength and integrity.

Six weeks later, Suzy lay dying. As her beloved daughter and other members of her family watched her fade and labor with her breathing, Suzy summoned up the energy to say, "I came into this world fighting for my life, fighting for my people and our culture. I am now leaving this world not needing to fight. . . . I've accomplished what I was set out for."

On April 2, 2006, Suzanne Rochon-Burnett died from lung disease. Her legacy of love, strength, and determination continues to inspire others to lead lives filled with respect and compassion.

Pauline Johnson-Tekahionwake

Few people who are trailblazers in their fields actually set out to change the world. Not everyone can pursue a passion or develop a childhood hobby into an interesting and important career. But (Emily) Pauline Johnson-Tekahionwake did just that.

She was born on March 10, 1861, on the Six Nations Indian Reserve, south of Brantford, Ontario—home to the Mohawks, the Oneidas, the Onondagas, the Cayugas, the Senecas, and the Tuscaroras. She was the

Pauline Johnson-Tekahionwake

youngest of George and Emily Johnson's four children.

Pauline's parents met when her mother traveled from her home in Ohio to visit her sister, Eliza, who was married to an Anglican missionary for the Six Nations on the Grand River Reserve. Emily and Eliza's father, Henry Howells, was a British educator who had moved his family from England and had instilled in his children respect for religion and a passion for reading. During her visit, Emily met George Johnson, a local Mohawk man employed as an interpreter for the Anglican church.

The romance and eventual marriage of a British-American white woman to a full-blooded Mohawk man created a lot of gossip. The newly married couple lived in a stately home called Chiefswood, which George had built on the Six Nations Reserve. Word spread that George was good at helping Natives and non-Natives settle disagreements. As a result, he got a job as an interpreter for the Six Nations Band Council and the Canadian government to ensure that local rules and laws were being followed by band members. Emily was content running her new household at Chiefswood and looking after her growing family.

Their youngest child, Pauline, was sickly and slept in her parents' bedroom until she was four. Her mother doted on her and allowed Pauline to have certain privileges that the other three Johnson children were never offered, such as having a pet chipmunk in the house. Pauline and her brother Allen were never sent to residential boarding school in London, Ontario, like her older sister Eva and brother Beverly.

Pauline's childhood was spent listening to the stories told by her father and her grandfather, John "Smoke" Johnson, as well as canoeing, reading, and riding the family pony. She attended the local residential school for two years but found it hard to relate to the other children. Pauline and her siblings had grown up at Chiefswood, the most luxurious home on the reserve, and had been pretty much isolated from other reserve children, so they were unaware of how different the living

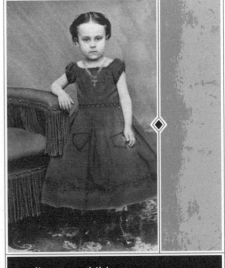

Pauline as a child.

conditions were for other families in the area. Also, English was the language spoken in her household, and Pauline never had the same struggles as her classmates, who were only just learning to read and write English.

When Pauline was fourteen, she and her brother Allen started to attend public school in Brantford, Ontario. Since Chiefswood was too far away for Pauline and Allen to go home to each day, they lived in Brantford with friends of their parents. This was Pauline's first time away from home, and she desperately missed the routine of life at Chiefswood—the hustle and bustle of people coming to speak with her father, the trips down the river in her beloved canoe, Wildcat, and the discussions of books and poetry with her mother.

It didn't take Pauline long to become familiar with her new home away from home, and her outgoing, confident personality attracted many new friends. What was once an intimidating town for the sheltered girl became a lively and fascinating place. Pauline was very fond of studying English and history, but she was most passionate about performing in school plays and poetry recitals. The two years at Brantford Central Collegiate passed quickly. Pauline graduated in 1877.

When she returned home to Chiefswood, Pauline realized that she was going to need a reason to return to Brantford on a regular basis. She missed the latest delights in the town's shop windows and the outings with her school friends.

Pauline as a teenager.

Pauline wanted to write and to see the world, but her family expected her to stay at home with her mother, learn how to run a household, and eventually marry. These expectations did not excite Pauline. She had tasted a bit of independence and freedom while she lived and went to school in Brantford. She longed to support herself by writing and dreamed of having her work published. This was not going to be easy, especially if she wanted to have support from her family. Her mother had very traditional beliefs about what a young woman like Pauline should and shouldn't do with her life, and Pauline knew that her mother would object to her writing ambitions.

A year after Pauline returned home to Chiefswood, her father was attacked while walking home from a Council meeting. George had been attacked twice before, because his efforts to stop the illegal timber trading on the reserve made him unpopular with those who were making money from the trade. His position of authority and his role as a law enforcer made George a target for those who were benefiting from breaking the law.

Pauline and her family were scared for George, but he was not about to be kept from doing his job for the Council or the government. He was driven to find those who were illegally trading trees, which belonged to the reserve, for alcohol. Pauline did her best to be of help to her mother, as Emily was under considerable stress from worrying about her husband and his health. Occasionally, Pauline got to leave the reserve and visit with friends in Brantford, but for the most part, she remained at Chiefswood wondering how and when she was going to start her life away from the reserve.

In 1884, six years after surviving the last attack on his life, Pauline's father died. The family was devastated and had to decide what to do with their home now that they no longer had George's income. Emily made the painful decision to rent out Chiefswood and move with Eliza and Pauline to a much smaller home in Brantford. Beverly and Allen were both working in the insurance industry, and Beverly sent money home when ever he could afford to.

The move to Brantford meant that Pauline now had the opportunity to join the local dramatic club and spend time with her girlfriends, many of them aspiring "new women." This idea of the "new woman" was a radically different point of view at the time and would come to be known as feminism—the belief that men and women should have the same economic, social, and political rights. Pauline longed to be a part of this new movement, a movement that upheld her right to pursue paid work.

Pauline as a young woman.

Knowing that she wanted to earn a living as a writer was her first step toward achieving that goal, but the next challenge was to have a piece of her work published. Pauline spent the next few years perfecting her writing skills. She was successful in having a number of her poems published in local, monthly publications, but not beyond her safe world of Brantford, Ontario. Pauline lacked the university education that most published poets of the day had, but despite this, she was driven to make a name for herself.

In 1892, Pauline was invited to Toronto to recite at An Evening with Canadian Authors, an event organized by an old friend from school. It was Pauline's first chance to show the elite of Canadian writers what she had to offer.

Pauline took to the stage with poise and confidence. She recited her poems from memory (unlike the other writers that night) and, through her words, offered the audience a glimpse into her world. She was proud of her British and Mohawk ancestry, and she knew that her perspective of both worlds was legitimate and unique.

The success of her recital in Toronto gave Pauline the publicity she needed to arrange a tour across Canada. She teamed up with music hall performer Owen Smily, and they crisscrossed the country over the next five years performing Pauline's comedy skits and plays. Pauline also gave recitals of her poetry. At the same time, Pauline wrote articles for various magazines, speaking passionately against the stereotypes given to Native women in the stories that were often published during this period.

In 1894, Pauline and Owen made their way to London, England. Pauline hoped to stir up enough interest with their shows to catch the attention of a publisher. Their efforts paid off, and Pauline published her first volume of poetry, *The White Wampum*, in 1895. Pauline's Mohawk name, *Tekahionwake* (pronounced dageh-eeon-wageh), means "double wampum," or "double life." She told British reporters that her last name of Johnson was only a baptismal name and that Tekahionwake was really her great-grandfather's name.

With a successful London trip under their belts, Pauline and Owen returned to Canada to continue their tours across the country. By 1897, Pauline was tired of traveling and wanted a place of her own to call home. She moved to Winnipeg, Manitoba, a young city that was accepting of people of mixed backgrounds—people like Pauline.

After one of her performances for her new home crowd in Winnipeg, Pauline was introduced to a local businessman named Charles Drayton. Charles was originally from Ontario, but his father had sent him to Winnipeg with the hope that the new business opportunities available in such a young city would appeal to him. Pauline was flattered by his attention, and the two eventually became engaged.

Then, Pauline received word that her mother was seriously ill. Pauline traveled home to Brantford, and soon after her arrival, her mother died. The death hit Pauline hard; to add to her woes, her engagement to Charles was called off.

Pauline threw herself into her work and started touring with a new partner, Walter McRaye. Walter was much younger than Pauline, but he idolized her and looked after all of their touring arrangements. Touring was hard work, and there was little or no time to enjoy the attractions of each stop along the

Pauline in winter.

way. Pauline and Walter worked throughout the seasons. When there was a storm that caused them to miss a connecting train and their show, they were still expected to pay for renting the theater or hall. It was difficult to make good money, and at forty-four, Pauline realized that she needed a steady income. Seeing that boys' adventure tales were very popular in the United States, Pauline submitted some of her own, like "The Wolfe Brothers," to a number of magazines and was able to earn a more secure wage from her writing than she was from touring.

In 1909, Pauline went to Vancouver, British Columbia, to take a vacation and rest from her hectic life. She loved Vancouver, with its beautiful views of the Pacific Ocean and the Rocky Mountains. During her London trip, Pauline had befriended Chief Joe Capilano, the outspoken Squamish chief from Vancouver, whose band lived on the North Shore. They met up again in Vancouver, and Chief Capilano took Pauline to his village and introduced her to his family. Pauline borrowed a canoe and spent much of her time paddling around the shores of Vancouver. The experience would inspire her to write one of her best-known poems, *The Lost Lagoon*:

"O! Lure of the Lost Lagoon,
I dream to-night that my paddle blurs
The purple shade where the seaweed stirs,
I hear the call of the singing firs
In the hush of the golden moon."

Pauline loved Vancouver so much that she decided to call the city home. She wrote for Vancouver's *Daily Province* magazine; many of her stories were legends of the Squamish people as told to her by Chief Capilano.

By 1910, Pauline could no longer ignore the fact that she had been feeling poorly for a long time, so she made an appointment to see a doctor. She was diagnosed with breast cancer, and as a result of her

Pauline Johnson-Tekahionwake

illness, she could no longer write on a regular basis. Her lifetime "easy come, easy go" attitude toward money meant that Pauline had never saved very much. Now that she was ill and unable to write as often as she used to, Pauline was broke. Her friends knew that she was too proud to accept charity, so they published a book of Pauline's Squamish folklore in 1911 and titled it *Legends of Vancouver.*

Pauline's last book was a success, and the money she earned from it was enough to give her peace of mind during her final days. Word had spread that the great Mohawk poet-performer was ill, and she was flooded with letters and visitors who wanted to express just how much they appreciated her stories and performances. Pauline died on March 7, 1913, just three days before her fifty-second birthday. She had shown the world that an unmarried woman could earn an independent living through her talent and hard work and that First Nations women had more to offer than the traditional roles in which they were cast.

Pauline Johnson-Tekahionwake's cremated remains were buried in Vancouver's majestic Stanley Park. She is the only local person ever to have been so honored.

Thocmetony (Sarah) Winnemucca

I t's no secret that life can be hard and people are often cruel. After a glance at the news today, you may feel like shrugging your shoulders and giving up on humanity and our troubled world. Thocmetony Winnemucca witnessed a tremendous amount of suffering and brutality during her time, but she never ceased her fight against injustice. Instead of bowing to oppression, she chose to lead her people and draw public awareness to the issues facing her community.

Thocmetony (Sarah) Winnemucca was born in 1844 in Nevada. Her grandfather, Truckee, was a respected leader of the Northern Paiute bands. A nomadic people, the Paiutes moved with each passing season. Sarah experienced a traditional childhood,

Thocmetony Winnemucca

harvesting nuts and other foods with the women while the men hunted and fished.

This time-honored way of life was disrupted, however, by the arrival of non-Native settlers to the area. They brought with them not only strange and disruptive new customs and habits, they also brought diseases like measles, tuberculosis, and typhoid fever. Accordingly, a great number of Paiutes—including two of Sarah's aunts—became sick and died. Meanwhile, Sarah's beloved forests dwindled as settlers chopped down trees for firewood and building materials.

Around the time she turned sixteen, Sarah's grandfather arranged for her and her younger sister, Elma, to study at the Academy of Notre Dame, a Roman Catholic mission school in San Jose, California. At first the sisters were enchanted by the novelty of their new surroundings. This excitement soon faded once they discovered that the other students' parents didn't want so-called savages at the school. Brought up to believe in the goodness of all people, Sarah and Elma were heartbroken by this cruel label.

Upon her return home, Sarah was horrified to learn that life had become even more difficult for the Paiutes. The new settlers had stolen the most fertile land, and greedy government agents from the Bureau of Indian Affairs grew fat from the resources set aside for the Paiutes. All turned a blind eye to the misery suffered by the Natives, who were dying from starvation, exposure, and disease.

Sarah's father felt desperate about the state of his people and put together a traveling stage show that he hoped would earn enough money to help feed and clothe the Paiutes. Sarah and Elma worked with their father, but the show was a flop. The family faced even tougher times when Sarah's mother and some other Paiutes were killed by ranchers who believed the Paiutes had stolen their livestock.

In 1868, Sarah found work as an interpreter for the U.S. Army at Fort McDermit. There she met a friendly officer named Edward C. Bartlett, and in 1871, married him in Salt Lake City, Utah. But married life was a disappointment. Sarah realized that Edward was an alcoholic, and after a few miserable weeks together, she left her husband and returned to Fort McDermit.

Sarah's father had moved, and in 1875, Sarah went to see him. She found a new job as an interpreter at the Malheur Reservation. Her boss, Indian agent Sam Parrish, behaved decently towards the Paiutes. He taught them how to grow crops and encouraged many to learn trades, such as carpentry, dam building, and blacksmithing, which might benefit the community. Best of all, a new school was built on the reservation, and Sarah became a teacher's assistant.

Unfortunately, only a year later, Sam Parrish was replaced by William Rinehart. Agent Rinehart was a vicious bully who abused many of the children and snatched away the crops that the Paiutes had sweated and slaved over. He also fired Sarah almost immediately. In the meantime, Sarah had fallen in love with Joseph Satwaller, and they left the Malheur Reservation and Rinehart far behind to begin a new life as husband and wife.

But Sarah's romance ended in bitter disillusionment once again, and she left Joseph to take a job doing housework near the John Day River. One day, she was visited by some Paiutes who asked her to speak on their behalf in Washington. Under Agent Rinehart, they told her, their people were starving to death. Someone had to make the government officials in Washington understand how bad things were for the Paiute bands. They also mentioned that a large group of Bannock Indians had left their reserve and were living with some Paiutes who had fled Malheur.

Sarah Winnemucca

Sarah quickly packed her things and left for Malheur to see the situation for herself. Before she could reach the reservation, however, the Bannock Indians declared war against the army. Sarah was informed that many Paiutes had sided with the army against the Bannocks and was warned that the Bannocks might attack her if she proceeded any further.

Many of the Paiute bands felt that the army had treated them with far more respect than the Bureau of Indian Affairs ever had, and they were hesitant to alienate any friendly non-Natives. Sarah likewise decided to help the army and volunteered to work as an army tracker. She left again for Malheur, learning on her journey there that her family, among other Paiutes, had been captured by the Bannocks. Eventually she helped many of these people escape. Sarah would later describe the work she did for the army during the Bannock War as "the hardest work I ever did for the government in all my life."

The end of the Bannock War did not spell peace and contentment for Sarah and the Paiute bands. Many Natives lost their lives after President Hayes forced the Paiutes to move to yet another reservation in the middle of a terrible, freezing winter. Enraged by the brutal neglect of her people, Sarah traveled to San Francisco, where she forcefully spoke against the Bureau of Indian Affairs and movingly described the abuses suffered by the Paiutes. Her gamble paid off, as many Americans were shocked and infuriated to hear of the mistreatment of Sarah's people.

In 1881, Sarah married Lewis H. Hopkins. She spent a good portion of her honeymoon lecturing and raising money for a trip to Washington, as she had faith that, once there, she could stir the congressmen's hearts to compassion for the Paiutes.

Sadly, her new husband gambled away all her earnings, and the trip had to be cancelled.

Later that year, Sarah's father died. The loss was difficult for her to endure, and she spent much of her time grieving in quiet reflection. Her father had always believed that people should do anything they could to make the world a better place. Sarah felt the same way, but with the recent disappointments in her personal life, she had lost a lot of her self-confidence. She wondered

Statue of Sarah in the U.S. Capitol National Statuary Hall.

what she, a Native woman with seemingly very little power, could do to ease the suffering of her fellow Paiutes.

Then inspiration struck. Sarah realized that she could reach many more people through her writing than she ever could with lectures. In 1883, Sarah became the first American Indian woman to publish a book. Titled *Life Among the Piutes: Their Wrongs and Claims*, it contained her impassioned cry for justice: "For shame! For shame! You dare cry out Liberty, when you hold us in places against our will, driving us from place to place as if we were beasts."

The book was a huge success, and Sarah tirelessly continued to demand fair treatment for her people.

Just as Sarah's professional life was taking off, her personal life became more difficult. In 1885, Sarah finally left Lewis, who had gambled away almost all of her hard-earned money, and moved to her brother Natchez's farm. Together they built a Paiute school, where she taught English, math, art, and Paiute history. The government would not support the school, though, and Sarah and Natchez had to close its doors a mere three years later.

On October 17, 1891, at the age of 47, Sarah died of tuberculosis in the comfort of her sister Elma's home. Where some people might have lost hope, Sarah had persevered, even in the face of overwhelming persecution from the ruling majority. Her activism, courage, and determination ensured that her people and their story would never be forgotten.

Maria Tallchief

You never know where life will take you when you consistently work hard at something you love. For a little girl from an Oklahoma reservation, talent and hard work put her in the spotlight on the world stage.

Elizabeth Marie Tallchief was born January 24, 1925, in Fairfax, Oklahoma. Her father, Alexander Tallchief, was an Osage Indian, and her mother, Ruth Porter Tallchief, was of Irish-Scottish descent. Betty Marie—as she was called by family and friends—lived with her parents, older brother Gerald, and younger sister Marjorie on the Osage Reservation.

The Osage Nation had become wealthy because there was oil on its land. Betty Marie's father didn't have to work, and there was extra money to send the Tallchief sisters to music and dance lessons. As a young child, Betty Marie had been fascinated with the dancing of the Osage tribe and had an excellent

Maria Tallchief

ear for music. Her mother had high hopes for all three children, and she set high standards for them.

By the age of five, Betty Marie had been taking dance lessons for a year and was said to be very strong for her age. She was also taking piano lessons, and her mother had dreams of her becoming a world-famous pianist.

The Tallchiefs wanted their children to have more opportunities, so they moved their family to Los Angeles, California, where their daughters could build upon the dance and music skills they had learned in Oklahoma. Moving away from family and friends was hard at first, but with time, they settled into their new life in the big city.

The two girls were kept very busy with school, music, and dance lessons. Their new ballet teacher, Ernest Belcher, felt that the girls hadn't been given adequate lessons by their former ballet instructor and said they would have to start learning again from scratch. The girls had been taught to dance on their toes at a very young age, and Mr. Belcher was surprised that Betty Marie and Marjorie hadn't injured themselves. It was going to take a lot of work to unlearn the techniques they had been taught in Oklahoma.

By the age of fifteen, Betty Marie was ready to move on to a new ballet teacher. She started working with a Russian instructor, Bronislava Nijinska, who was very well respected in the dance community. Madame Nijinska reminded her students to think like dancers at all times and hold themselves like dancers, even if they were only waiting for the bus.

Her philosophy was that a dancer is *always* a dancer, not just when she happens to be in the dance studio or on stage. She taught them that ballet is art, and the dancer is a part of it at all times. Betty Marie listened and learned, and after graduating from high school at age seventeen, she decided to move to New York City. There she auditioned successfully for the Ballet Russe de Monte Carlo, where her talent, strong work ethic, and striking good looks made her a young performer to watch. She was passionate about giving her best with each performance, and her reputation grew as she was given featured solos while the company toured the country.

One day, Sergei Denham, the director of the Ballet Russe, brought up the subject of Betty Marie's name. He knew that she was incredibly talented, but he felt she was more likely to become a dancing legend if she had a more traditional stage name. Betty Marie was torn, as she longed to have her career take off but wasn't willing to sacrifice who she was, a Tallchief. She was very proud of her mixed heritage and wasn't willing to change her surname just because the ballet world had never known a Native American dancer. She changed her first name to Maria, however, as there were other Elizabeths and Maries in the company already.

In 1944, George Balanchine, a famous Russian choreographer who had come to America in 1933, became the resident choreographer for the Ballet Russe. He saw potential for further greatness in Maria and decided to take her under his wing. Her ability soon won her leading roles in Balanchine's ballets. In 1946, Maria Tallchief and George Balanchine married.

The couple traveled to France and worked with the Paris Opera Ballet. Maria was the first American to dance with the company in more than one hundred years. Up until this time, many Europeans had believed that the best dancers came only from Europe or Russia. They didn't believe an American could be considered one of the world's most talented dancers. Maria proved them wrong; they loved her performances.

After a hugely successful stint in Europe, Maria and George returned home to New York City. Maria became the prima ballerina in George's new company, the Ballet Society (later renamed the New York City Ballet). Her performances helped to bring fame and respect to American ballet.

By this time, Maria was often giving eight performances a week, and her whole life revolved around ballet. She began to feel that there should be more to life than just work. She wanted to start a family, but George didn't think that would be good for her career. Eventually the couple divorced, but they continued to work together for many years.

Maria's career as a dancer had earned her honors and fame around the world. In 1953, president Dwight D. Eisenhower declared her Woman of the Year, and she was also honored by the state of Oklahoma and given the name *Wa-Xthe-Thomba*, which means "woman of two worlds." She had successfully turned her childhood dream of becoming a dancer into a reality.

In 1965, Maria shocked the dance world by announcing her retirement at the age of forty-one. She was still in her prime, but having remarried and become a mother, Maria felt it was more important to be at home with her daughter while she was young than to be touring and missing out on family life in Chicago.

Although she had retired from dancing, Maria remained connected to the dance world, and in 1974 she accepted a position as artistic director of the Lyric Opera Company in Chicago. Her first act was to put together a group of dancers who would work with the opera company. It was a wonderful experience for her, and she relished being surrounded by her two passions: music and dance.

In 1980, the Lyric Opera Company and the Lyric Ballet Company separated, and Maria cofounded the Chicago City Ballet Company. Her younger sister, Marjorie, had also become a famous ballerina and had spent many years in Paris. The two sisters now came together to develop a company that would reflect their integrity, talent, and passion.

Maria was recognized for her outstanding talent and lifelong dedication when she became a Kennedy Center honoree at the 1996 Washington, D.C., gala. The little girl from the Osage Nation had grown up to become one of the most celebrated and talented artists America had ever produced. Her achievements are also her people's achievements, and that's something everyone can celebrate.

Wilma Mankiller

Remaining positive about life is a gift you can give to yourself. When you're able to find the good in a bad situation, you've triumphed over that challenge and grown as an individual. Wilma Pearl Mankiller, social and political activist, never let the tough times defeat her. She used her self-determination, self-confidence, and integrity to survive the hard times in her life and help her people.

Wilma was born November 18, 1945, in Tahlequah, Oklahoma, into a large and loving family. She was the sixth of eleven children born to Charles and Irene Mankiller. The family lived at Mankiller Flats, a parcel of land located in eastern Oklahoma, in the heart of Cherokee Nation.

Wilma's family didn't have a lot of money. Their small house lacked the modern-day conveniences that we now take for granted. They lived without indoor plumbing, electricity, and central heating.

Wilma Mankiller

The children had to haul water and cut wood, but they learned that life is balanced when you're in tune with the natural world.

Wilma's parents wanted to offer their children a chance to grow up with more choices than they had been given. Like so many other Native Americans, most Cherokees were living in extreme poverty, and few had access to clean drinking water, safe housing, or a chance to further their education.

Then the U.S. government came up with a plan to encourage Native Americans to move off their reservations and into cities across the country. By promising access to better jobs, schools, and housing conditions in the cities, the government thought it could solve many problems for the people living on the reserves. Wilma's parents were torn. They loved their community, and it was important to them to be close to their extended families, but they were tempted by the promises of the government.

Wilma's parents finally decided to leave their home in Oklahoma and move their family to San Francisco, California. Eleven-year-old Wilma was upset at leaving behind the only home she had ever known. When her family made it to San Francisco, they were disappointed to find out that the promises of the Bureau of Indian Affairs had been hollow.

Back in Oklahoma, Wilma had attended school in a little three-room schoolhouse where her fellow students were all Cherokee children. Now that she lived in San Francisco, Wilma experienced what it felt like to be a visible minority living in a predominately non-Native world. She knew firsthand what it was like having others make fun of her accent, her last name, and her appearance. On her way to school, she walked past signs in shop windows that stated, "No dogs, no Indians."

Wilma sought strength in the history of her people. She started to think her family's resettlement to California was like the Cherokee's historical forced resettlement known as the Trail of Tears. In 1830, president Andrew Jackson had signed the Indian Removal Act, which stated that many Native Americans would be moved off of their land so that white settlers could have it. Thousands of Native people across the United States were forced to move from their ancestral homes. Most of the Cherokees had ignored the Indian Removal Act. In 1838, president Martin Van Buren sent the army in to round up the Cherokees like they were livestock. Those who refused to leave were shot. Thousands died along the way, as many of the wagons broke and people were forced to walk 1,200 miles west to Oklahoma, their new home.

Wilma identified now with those people who had been forced to leave their homes, but she found hope at the San Francisco Indian Center. It was a gathering spot for local Native families who were looking for a way to help deal with their relocation disappointments. The center gave them a sense of community and purpose.

When Wilma graduated from high school in 1963, she got an office job working for a finance company. Then, just days before her eighteenth birthday, she got married. Nine months later she was a mother, and by the time she was twenty-one, Wilma had two daughters.

The decade of the 1960s was a time of great change. People were more vocal about the injustices that existed in the world. African-Americans were fighting for their civil rights, women were fighting for equality between the sexes, and Native Americans were fighting for their ancestral lands to be returned to them. San Francisco was the home base for many groups that were working toward greater social awareness, and Wilma found herself drawn to many of these new ideas that championed the rights of those who were in the minority.

In 1969, a group of Native Americans took over Alcatraz Island, home of the infamous federal penitentiary, which had operated until 1963. The group wanted to draw attention to the ongoing problems that their people on reservations were facing throughout the country. Native Americans were living in poverty, and the government wasn't honoring the treaties it had signed with Native communities. Wilma supported the occupation of Alcatraz, and she was motivated to learn more about how to help her community back in Oklahoma.

Fifteen years after she and her family had packed up their belongings for the move to San Francisco, Wilma returned to Oklahoma. Her father had died from kidney disease and was to be buried in Oklahoma. Wilma drove home to attend the funeral. She found that even fifteen years of separation had not

changed the deep connection she felt to her home-
land and to her Cherokee people.

Once back in California, Wilma decided to attend
San Francisco State University. Wilma had never
thought about going to a university when she was in
public school, but her involvement with the Alcatraz
incident had built her self-esteem. She realized that
if she wanted to be of service to her people, she needed to learn more skills that would help her solve the
problems in her community.

Wilma was excited about the prospect of moving
back to Oklahoma after attending university. Her
husband, however, was not. He wanted Wilma to be
a traditional stay-at-home wife in California. They
divorced, and in 1977, Wilma moved back to Oklahoma with her daughters. She began working with
the community and explored ways to obtain grants to
start up community projects.

Two years later, as Wilma was driving into Tahlequah, she was involved in a head-on crash with a car
that had been traveling in the wrong direction in her
lane. The accident killed the other driver and nearly
cost Wilma her own life. It proved to be a life-chang-
ing experience. Although Wilma's body was broken,
her spirit was not. Despite going through almost
twenty operations and recovering at home, she was
still able to focus on the positive things in her life. By
following the Cherokee slogan "to be of a good mind,"
she was able to devote her energies to finding solu-
tions to the housing and water shortages that
plagued her community.

By 1981, Wilma was ready to tackle her first big community project. Working with the nearby community of Bell, Wilma, along with activist Charlie Soap (whom she married in 1986), helped to motivate and organize local people into building their own waterline. In effect, Wilma brought back the old tradition of a community working together for the benefit of everyone.

Wilma was then asked to work with other Native American communities to help them help themselves. With the success of her community projects, Wilma was encouraged to get involved with politics. In 1983, Chief Ross Swimmer asked Wilma to run as his deputy chief in the next Cherokee Nation election. After some initial hesitation, she decided to run and was elected.

By 1985, Chief Swimmer had taken a new job in Washington, D.C., and Wilma Mankiller took over as chief. Wilma was elected to the position in 1987 and again in 1991 and made history by being the Cherokees' first elected female chief. She was now responsible for almost 140,000 people and a $70 million annual budget. "Prior to my election," she said, "young Cherokee girls would never have thought that they might grow up and become chief."

Wilma has received eighteen honorary doctorate degrees from different universities. She has been honored with inductions into the National Women's Hall of Fame, the Oklahoma Women's Hall of Fame, and the International Women's Hall of Fame. She has also been awarded the Presidential Medal of Freedom—

America's greatest civilian honor. Wilma has had the opportunity to meet presidents Ronald Reagan, George H. W. Bush, and Bill Clinton at the White House. Remarkably, she is a survivor of two kidney transplants, one donated from her eldest brother and the other by her niece.

Although Wilma Mankiller is now retired from politics, she continues to serve as a spokesperson for her people through her lectures, writings, and media interviews. By remaining true to the Cherokee way of always striving to remain positive, through good times and bad, she has helped to revitalize her community and others across the country.

Mary Kim Titla

Living your life so that you feel good about who you are is often tough to do. There are daily pressures from school, home life, and friends, and these are often overwhelming. It's important to remember that you are at your best when you are able to listen to your inner voice and follow your passions.

Mary Kim Titla is an example of someone who strives for balance in all aspects of her life. She was born on November 24, 1960, in San Carlos, Arizona, home to the San Carlos Apache Tribe. She is the eldest of the five children born to Charlotte and Phillip Titla, including her siblings Millie, Phillip Darrell, Phillip Jr., and Gussie.

Mary Kim's paternal grandparents lived with the family, and they helped to keep an eye on their grandchildren while Phillip and Charlotte were away at work. There was a lot to keep the children busy at home, including playing with the chickens, dogs, and horses.

Mary Kim Titla

Their house may have been small, and they lived without indoor plumbing and electricity for many years, but Mary Kim didn't feel like they were lacking anything. Theirs was a loving home filled with messages of hope and a belief that education would be their key to future successes.

Charlotte and Phillip Titla worked very hard to send their children to boarding schools, because they wanted the best possible education for them. During school breaks, the family would go on road

Mary Kim *(at top)* with *(from left to right)* her father Phillip, sister Millie, and her mother Charlotte.

trips to explore the western United States. Mary Kim's parents wanted to show their children that their world extended beyond the reservation and that there were endless possibilities if they were able to get an education and work hard.

Mary Kim at the top of a pyramid in high school.

The Titla children were brought up to believe that it is possible to break the cycle of poverty, abuse, and violence that plague many Native American communities. They learned at an early age that if people respect themselves, they will respect the larger world in which they live.

When Mary Kim was in high school, she was involved in an incident that taught her a valuable lesson. She was joyriding with friends in a pickup truck that was traveling too fast. The friend who was driving lost control of the truck while turning a corner, and Mary Kim injured her neck and back. Luckily, there was a group of people nearby who saw the accident, and they helped get Mary Kim and her four friends out of the truck, which had rolled over. Because of her injuries, Mary Kim had to attend public school for the eleventh grade so she could be closer to home and the assistance of her parents. She learned to listen to her inner voice and say no to others who wanted her to try things she wasn't comfortable doing.

Mary Kim knew that after completing high school she was going to go to college. She started researching the different scholarships that were available, and she noticed that many Native American pageants awarded scholarships to their winners. She entered the Miss National Congress of American Indians Pageant in 1981. She traveled to Alaska for the competition and met many wonderful young Native American women from across the country. Mary Kim won the pageant, and she was awarded a scholarship for school. She also had the opportunity to travel across the country representing the National Congress of American Indians (NCAI) organization.

Mary Kim in high school.

When Mary Kim was growing up, she always wanted to be a teacher. Now that she was finally enrolled in college, she found that she was drawn to journalism (the work of collecting, writing, and reporting news) and photography. She kept extremely busy by participating in the Native American Club, working on the school newspaper, and serving on the yearbook committee.

She transferred from junior college to attend the University of Oklahoma to pursue a degree in journalism.

Soon after starting her studies, Mary Kim met an Assiniboine/Paiute man by the name of John Mosley. John grew up in California and had recently transferred to the University of Oklahoma, too. They started dating and eventually started talking about getting married.

John traveled to Mary Kim's parents' house and asked them for their permission to wed their daughter.

Mary Kim in college.

Phillip and Charlotte said no to John's request; they wanted Mary Kim to finish her university courses first. John was eager to wed Mary Kim, but he respected her family's wishes and went back to Oklahoma. When John and Mary Kim graduated, John returned to Mary Kim's parents' house and asked them a second time if he could wed their daughter. Phillip and Charlotte knew that Mary Kim wanted to pursue a graduate degree, and they asked John to wait until Mary Kim had finished her two-year program. John left the Titla home undaunted, as he knew the day would come when they would give their consent. He could wait a little while longer.

After dating for five years, Mary Kim and John wed a few months before she finished her master's degree in mass communication from Arizona State University. They were soon blessed with the birth of their first son, Jordan, in December 1985. In a short period of time, Mary Kim had become a wife and mother, and she was looking for her first job in journalism.

The U.S. job market was still suffering from a slowdown in the economy (a recession) during the mid-1980s. Although Mary Kim was highly qualified to start working as a journalist, she wasn't able to find work in her chosen field. Slightly discouraged but not without hope, she applied for a receptionist position at a local news station. While interviewing for the job, she mentioned that she hoped to use her starting position within the company as a way to break into a trainee reporter's position later on.

By 1987, Mary Kim got her first on-air break by covering the visit of the late Pope John Paul II. The Pope had traveled to Arizona to speak with Native American leaders, and Mary Kim was able to rely on the relationships that she had made with tribal leaders during her year-long tour as Miss NCAI to offer on-air coverage of the event.

During the next eighteen years, Mary Kim had two more children, and she continued working as a TV news reporter in Arizona. She has been honored with numerous awards, including being inducted into the Cronkite Hall of Fame at Arizona State University. She has also received first-place awards from the Associated Press, Arizona Press Club, and the Native

Mary Kim Titla, journalist.

American Journalists Association for her television news reporting. Mary Kim has remained connected to her community by working with Native American youth; she was honored for these efforts with an Ira Hayes Honorable Warrior Award, a tribute that celebrates those who have given outstanding service to their community and country.

Being the mother of three teenage boys for whom daily computer use is the norm, Mary Kim decided to search the Internet to see what was available for Native youth online. She found that there was very little on the Internet that was positive, and this gave her the idea to start an online magazine that would allow young Native people to have a voice of their own. With her three boys acting as the magazine's advisors, Mary Kim initiated NativeYouthMagazine.com.

The e-magazine features stories and pictures from Native youth throughout the United States and Canada. As publisher, Mary Kim has created an environment that is similar to the one in which she grew up, where anything can be discussed and youth are given many positive role models.

With the successful start-up of her e-magazine, Mary Kim decided to expand her newfound passion and established Titla Consulting, a company that specializes in media relations and motivational speaking. She is now busy traveling to other communities, spreading the message to youth that they can achieve what they are passionate about if they're willing to work hard and be true to themselves.

In January 2007, Mary Kim completed her first half-marathon race (approximately thirteen miles, or twenty-one kilometers). She has been a runner for most of her adult life and grew up watching her mother run on the San Carlos airstrip. Mary Kim has always believed in the harmony that can be achieved by balancing the physical, emotional, mental, and spiritual aspects of life. Running is a great way for her to tap into her inner self and achieve a sense of peace with her body, mind, and soul.

Never one to shy away from hard work, Mary Kim has earned a reputation as a person of integrity. As a teenager, she volunteered for the United National Indian Tribal Youth (UNITY), a nonprofit organization that emphasizes good citizenship for youth through community service. Her leadership efforts gained her national attention when she became the first Native American to earn the Congressional Award Gold Medal, the highest honor given by the U.S. Congress in acknowledgement of the accomplishments of youth in their communities and in personal development and physical fitness.

As a Native woman who has achieved so much in her life, Mary Kim has become a role model for many people. Encouraged by the support of people in her community, she announced in May 2007 that she would be running for a seat in Arizona's First Congressional District. One of her goals is to see young people become more active in their communities, because as Mary Kim knows, when you get involved you can't help but care.

Mary Kim's positive outlook on life and many accomplishments make it exciting to see what else this dynamic woman will achieve during the next phase of her life.

Lorna B. Williams

Your shoes were made in China. You play online chess against a friend in India. You buy comic books that come all the way from Japan. Welcome to the world of globalization. The more our diverse cultures are thrown together—over the Internet, in the worlds of commerce and politics, or through the arts, media, and literature—the more we require cultural understanding and education to keep our separate traditions alive. Lorna B. Williams, a world leader in Aboriginal teaching, aims to explore these differences and maintain a unique cultural identity for Natives as well as all peoples of the world.

Lorna was born prematurely on September 27, 1947, in Mount Currie, British Columbia, on the west coast of Canada. In keeping with the traditions of her people, the Lil'wat First Nation, the delivery was facilitated by a group of women from her village. They used time-honored natural remedies to ease the tiny baby girl through her first difficult days in

Lorna B. Williams

the world. Though she remained a sickly child, this tight-knit and supportive community helped give Lorna strength.

Lorna grew up in a huge family with eleven rambunctious brothers and sisters. The Williams' home was always open to any other child who might want to live with them and learn new skills. Certainly, Lorna's parents had much to teach: George Williams possessed keen business skills and also taught the youngsters how to trap, farm, and fish. His wife, Adelina Williams, shared her knowledge of herbs and natural remedies. Unsurprisingly, the Williams' home was a crowded and friendly place, filled with the sounds of instruction and laughter.

Growing up in this warm and encouraging environment, it was only natural that Lorna became interested in learning more about her mother's passions: medicine and the healing arts. She confidently enrolled in a nursing program but was surprised and disappointed to learn that the non-Native medical system failed to live up to her ideals. Compared to traditional holistic healing, Western medicine seemed cold and clinical, and Lorna could not see herself thriving in the field.

Undeterred, Lorna took a job as a home-school coordinator, acting as a liaison between local schools, districts, and their communities. She soon discovered that most non-Native people didn't really understand First Nations children or their culture. She saw that the educational system wasn't catering to their needs, and First Nations children were having a tough time trying to adapt to non-Native teaching methods. Lorna gained many insights into how the system was failing First Nations students during this time.

She moved to a new position at the University of British Columbia, where she was responsible for finding safe homes and schools for approximately eighty First Nations students who had moved to Vancouver from remote, rural communities. The youths under her care were from different Aboriginal cultures, and Lorna's insight expanded as she learned more about diversity among First Nations peoples.

A year later, Lorna took a job as a group leader with Canada World Youth, an organization that provides young people from the ages of seventeen to twenty-four with opportunities to learn employable skills in Canada and overseas. Accompanied by a group of ten Canadian youths, Lorna embarked on a journey to Malaysia.

Malaysia is located in Southeast Asia and is a country of great cultural diversity, populated by 25 million people of Malay, Chinese, Indigenous, and Indian descent. Lorna found her time in Malaysia somewhat unsettling. When she was a child, she had often felt angry because she could not understand why her elders had not protected her people, territory, and traditions from colonization. In Malaysia, however, Lorna met Indigenous people who were at a similar stage of colonization as her grandparents' generation had been. She saw that small, unremarkable changes to these communities added up over time to a complete breakdown of tradition. Before long, the minority culture would be swallowed up, or assimilated, by the majority culture. Finally, Lorna understood why her people had found it difficult to resist the slow and seemingly harmless erosion of their civilization.

Once she was back home in Mount Currie, Lorna decided to combat assimilation by living like her ancestors had in a practice called *Ucwalmicw Tmicw*, which means "the people and the land are one." She borrowed a tent from one of her brothers and employed her ancestors' hand-logging techniques to build a log house. Living off the land, Lorna began to reflect on her profound experiences working with youth. She concluded that it was time to focus her efforts on education and young people.

Lorna's experience in Malaysia had shown her that in order to keep their cultures alive, Natives had to take control of their destinies and advance understanding of their own traditions. She developed the idea of a community-based school and created a program that showed teachers how to relate to Native children and adolescents. Because many First Nations communities have experienced a decline in the number of members who can speak a Native language, Lorna wanted the instructors at the school to teach bilingually. She also recommended that they explain the Lil'wat First Nation's side of history rather than the local history found in textbooks, which was usually written from a non-Native perspective. Lorna's innovative program, developed in conjunction with Simon Fraser University, was a tremendous success: after years of misunderstanding and neglect from administrators and instructors, educators could at last fulfill the needs of a community and help to build cultural pride.

Today, Lorna Williams is an assistant professor and the director of Aboriginal teacher education at the University of Victoria in British Columbia. She also holds a Canada Research Chair in Indigenous knowledge and learning, a position of honor bestowed on the brightest of Canadian academics who work at expanding knowledge in their fields. Her tireless work to promote cultural understanding inspired her to write *Exploring Mount Currie*, a social studies book for students in the second grade. She also codirected *First Nations: The Circle Unbroken*, an educational video series, and has taught instructional methods around the world. Lorna has received the Outstanding Teacher Award, the Dedicated to Kids Award, and the Order of British Columbia, the province's highest award for outstanding achievement by one of its residents.

Lorna Williams continues to inspire others with her passion to see First Nations cultures thrive in a globalized world. Only through understanding and education will we be able to maintain our cultural identities. This fearless educator is taking steps to ensure that the ancient traditions will live on.

Susan Aglukark

Inuit singer and songwriter Susan Aglukark has a message she would like everyone to believe: you are your own most powerful source of strength. But she knows it's not easy to hang on to this belief, especially when life throws some ugly experiences at you.

Susan Aglukark was born in Churchill, Manitoba, on January 27, 1967, the fourth of seven children. Her parents are both ordained ministers of the Pentecostal church. The family moved to different places in the North for a number of years before settling in the small community of Arviat on the west coast of the Hudson Bay, in the territory of Nunavut.

Living in Canada's Far North, Susan knows what it is like to come of age in a community that is largely ignored by the rest of the world. Aboriginal communities may be isolated, but that isolation does not protect them. Instead, the sense of being ignored by the rest of society can lead to feelings of desperation

Susan Aglukark

and loneliness. As a child, Susan witnessed the everyday effects that despair has on a community.

She sought refuge by writing poems and pouring her innermost thoughts onto the pages of her journal. Susan found that her writings gave her an outlet and a sense of belonging.

When she was nine years old, Susan was sexually abused by a family acquaintance. Aside from telling her mother, she spoke to no one about it until she went public with her story thirteen years later. She found the strength to move on with her life in her faith, in her family, and in herself. She was determined not to let this terrible experience define her life and who she was.

The teen years were hard for Susan. In addition to experiencing the usual teenage struggles with identity, hormones, and uncertainty about the future, she had to deal with leaving home at fifteen to attend high school in Iqualuit. For Susan, living in a new place without her family and being surrounded by strangers in a new school environment were very difficult.

Since many Inuit communities are small and isolated, schools are spread out and children often have to leave their homes to continue their schooling. Many don't graduate from high school, because without proper support, the move from one's home community to the next to attend school is too difficult. As a young girl, Susan's own mother had been taken from her grandmother's home and was flown to mission house to attend school. Not wanting to live in a boarding school, cut off from the familiar pattern of her old life, this twelve-year-old child walked home across the tundra alone. It was no small wonder that Susan herself felt uncomfortable at her new school and, after just three months, returned home.

Realizing that she would have more opportunities in life if she finished her high school education, Susan tried again; this time she moved to Yellowknife, Northwest Territories. It was there that she seriously began to hope for a career as a singer/songwriter. Inspired by a conversation she had with a friend about the need to belong, Susan wrote her first song at the age of seventeen. Lights had to be out at 10:00 p.m. at her boarding school, but Susan was too inspired to go to bed, so she sneaked into the bathroom and wrote the song "Searching" while sitting in a bathtub.

After completing high school, Susan moved to Canada's capital, Ottawa, and got a government job in the Department of Indian and Northern Affairs. She worked as a translator and later as an executive assistant to the president of an Inuit lobbying group. Despite having a day job, Susan started pursuing her musical passions in her free time. She had produced an independent album, *Arctic Rose*, which was hugely popular with listeners in the North. She didn't have much experience performing in public, but word had already spread across the North that Susan was an incredibly talented artist.

The Canadian Broadcasting Corporation (CBC) was putting together a CD of eastern Arctic performers, and they had been told that they needed to check out a rising star named Susan Aglukark. The CBC contacted Susan and asked her for a copy of her music. After hearing her sing, the producers at the CBC asked Susan if she wanted to work with them. She heartily agreed and the result was the 1992 compilation release of the CD *Dreams for You.*

Soon after finishing her project with the CBC, Susan began working on bringing her song "Searching" to life as a music video. The video aired on TV and quickly became a favorite with viewers, going on to win an award for outstanding cinematography.

EMI Music Canada had signed Susan to a record deal in 1993, and they re-released her album *Arctic Rose.* By the end of the year, she had also produced her *Christmas* album. Before the record deal, Susan's albums had been sold mainly by mail order across the North, but with the re-release of *Arctic Rose* and the success of her debut music video, consumers across Canada were now eagerly snapping up her albums.

In 1994, she attended the National Aboriginal Achievement Awards ceremony and blew away the audience with her performance—in the Inuktitut language—of the hymn "Amazing Grace." Later that evening, Susan was honored with an Aboriginal Achievement Award for her ongoing work with First Nations youth and for her musical achievements.

Susan released her next album, *This Child*, in 1995. The album got radio play on pop, country, and easy-listening stations. Her clear, strong vocals, combined with her unforgettable melodies and thoughtful lyrics, were more than enough to earn her a place in the history books as the first Inuk performer to have a hit in the Top 40. Her first single, titled "O Siem," sings the praises of seeing one's family and friends; it would go on to reach number one on the Canadian pop charts, and the album would reach triple platinum status in Canada, selling 300,000 copies.

Susan began touring across the country, and after her performances she often stayed behind to meet with local groups of sexual-abuse victims. Susan is a role model to many, especially for those who have also suffered abuse. She is living proof that no one has to be held back by such experiences, although she hasn't always felt so self-assured. It was through writing music and remaining true to her faith in God and herself that she was able to slowly pull herself away from despair and embrace the beauty in life. Her message to young people is simple: believe in yourself and don't be afraid to do what you want to do.

In 1999, Susan released *Unsung Heroes*. It had taken her nearly two years to put the album together, partially because she was busy raising her son, Cameron, and partially because she wanted to take the necessary time to produce an album that reflected her maturing sound and lyrics. Her previous albums had focused on themes from her life and those of her people. With *Unsung Heroes*, the focus was more on universal themes that non-Inuit and Inuit alike can relate to.

Life for a recording artist is busy enough, but Susan is also dedicated to her work as a motivational speaker for youth. She regularly crisscrosses the country giving self-esteem workshops that help young Aboriginal people learn how they can cope with the feelings of loss. Susan knows that it's possible to turn these negative feelings around, and by helping young First Nations people focus on "reawakening" their self-esteem, she offers them and their communities hope for the future.

Although she has lived in the city and in the spotlight for many years, Susan hasn't turned her back on her Inuit traditions. She grew up learning how to prepare the meat of animals that her parents caught, as well as the techniques for cleaning the hides. No part of an animal is wasted, and Susan, like generations of Inuit women before her, learned how to sew and decorate these valued hides. She still enjoys camping with her family and credits her Arctic camping trips with bringing balance and perspective to her busy urban life.

You might think such a celebrated artist would slow down after releasing four hugely successful albums in a few short years, but not Susan. In 2002, she released her fifth album, *Big Feeling*. This was followed by *Blood Red Earth* in 2006. She has won three Juno Awards (Canada's equivalent to a Grammy),

performed for audiences around the world, and been
made an officer of the Order of Canada, Canada's
highest civilian honor, which celebrates Canadians
who have made a major difference to their country.
Perhaps even more importantly, she has inspired
countless children to believe in themselves and their
dreams.

Winona LaDuke

Politics shape the way we live and slant our outlook on the world. While we can all agree on the importance of having our say, it's easy to feel detached from, bored by, or disillusioned with the political process. As a Native woman accustomed to broken promises and neglect from the government, Winona LaDuke was uncertain about her role in the political landscape. It was by using her passion for public speaking and activism, however, that she was able to empower her people and give them a more public voice.

Winona came from a fervently political background. Her father, Vincent "Sun Bear" LaDuke, was from the Anishinaabeg reservation of White Earth in northern Minnesota. From an early age, he'd rallied against the loss of White Earth territory to non-Natives. Disturbed by the apparent complacency among his people and the lack of opportunities in the logging community, he set off for Washington, D.C.,

Winona LaDuke

armed with only a handmade sign that read "Have Blanket, Will Travel."

Vincent's sign wasn't meant to be funny. It referred to the way the government has forced Natives to move from place to place, off their homelands, against their will. This sign, as well as Vincent's charisma, seized the attention of Betty Bernstein, a young Russian-Jewish artist from New York. Both shared a passion for activism, and soon enough, a passion for each other. The couple married in 1958, and daughter Winona was born a year later in Los Angeles, California.

There was no happily-ever-after for Betty and Vincent. They split up when Winona was five years old, and she and her mother moved to Oregon. Winona's new home was vastly different from the one she had known in culturally diverse Los Angeles. Her mixed heritage made her stand out in an otherwise all-white town. Native American history was rarely discussed in her classes, and when it was, indigenous people were often portrayed as "obstacles" to civilization. But Winona didn't let her outsider status drag her down in self-pity; instead, she joined her high school debate team, which won six consecutive state championships.

Not long after starting college, Winona heard Cherokee activist Jimmy Durham deliver an impassioned speech on Native rights. His fiery words inspired her to take time off from her studies at Harvard University and help Native groups in the Southwest protest the mining of uranium on their land. Her interviews and fiery speeches earned her the nickname of "No Nukes LaDuke," and at the young age of eighteen, she addressed the United Nations on the mining issues facing many Native lands.

In 1982, Winona graduated from Harvard with a degree in Native economic development and moved to her father's hometown, White Earth. Though enrolled as a member of the Anishinaabeg band, Winona had never visited the reservation before and knew very few people there. White Earth nonetheless felt like home, and she gladly accepted a job as the reservation's high school principal while

Winona LaDuke

researching her master's thesis on the reservation's subsistence economy.

It didn't take Winona long to realize that the community was facing a massive crisis in the shape of a land dispute with the federal government. A court ruled that land had indeed been taken illegally from the Anishinaabeg (land that had been promised them in the White Earth Treaty of 1867), but added that the people were more than one hundred years too late in filing a lawsuit to recover their land. With that announcement, the court dismissed the peoples' case.

Winona and the residents of White Earth were outraged. Most Anishinaabeg people could not read or write English during the 1800s and certainly had not had educated lawyers to see that they were treated fairly. In response to the ruling, Winona created the White Earth Land Recovery Project. Its goal is to recover reservation land controlled by non-Native people. So far the group has reclaimed about 1,500 acres and is still going strong today.

In addition to reclaiming the land that was taken from her people, Winona is dedicated to educating the Anishinaabeg about the importance of protecting the land and the environment. With half of White Earth's population living in poverty, it can sometimes be difficult to convince people to refrain from slashing down trees for money. By educating the community's children, Winona believes they'll come to understand why it's important to know where wood comes from, how long it takes for a tree to grow, the relationship a tree has with the forest and the animals that live in it, and how wood can be harvested selectively, without clear-cutting an entire forest. By teaching others about the long-term benefits of a healthy planet, she hopes to leave future generations with a greater respect and appreciation for nature.

In 1996, Winona was approached by the Green Party to run as presidential-hopeful Ralph Nader's vice presidential running mate. She turned him down at first. She was pregnant with her third child, and besides, she didn't feel connected to federal politics.

After all, politicians have made a variety of promises to Natives, many of which have never been kept. Winona wasn't certain that she wanted to join their ranks. On the other hand, she knew that decisions made in Washington would affect both her life and the lives of those she loved. She decided to accept the challenge and ran for office in 1996 and 2000. Though she lost both times, Winona believed that winning was less important than drawing attention to the needs of Native American communities and making the public aware of the lack of Native representation in Washington.

Winona LaDuke with students.

Somehow Winona has also found the time to write seven books, including *Last Standing Woman*, a historical novel about her people, and *All Our Relations: Native Struggles for Land and Life*, a nonfiction account of Native resistance to the destruction of the environment. Her other titles include *Marxism and Native Americans, Recovering the Sacred: The Power of Naming and Claiming, New Perspectives on Environmental Justice: Gender, Sexuality, and Activism*, and her children's books *The Sugar Bush* and *The Winona LaDuke Reader: A Collection of Essential Writings*. Winona has also contributed to and coauthored many more books.

She continues to use her talents for public speaking, organizing, and activism, to open up politics to everyone in America, not just the well-heeled white men who have historically dominated the government. Winona LaDuke is helping her people regain their voice and ensuring that they will always play an active part in shaping their own destiny.

Sandra Lovelace Nicholas

As most Aboriginal communities in Canada are not well represented within the federal government, it is often difficult for them—especially for the women—to be heard by the non-Native politicians. Fortunately for the Maliseet people of the Tobique First Nation in New Brunswick, they have senator Sandra Lovelace Nicholas to represent them.

Sandra was born April 15, 1948. Her small community, situated near the Maine/New Brunswick border, was established by the British government at the turn of the nineteenth century. Before colonization and the establishment of a reserve, the day-to-day activities of the Maliseet people revolved around maintaining their way of life and their independence.

The community's existence depended upon the cooperation of its members to share resources. Everyone was able to help out in some way, regardless of age, gender, or abilities. The same was true for

Sandra Lovelace Nicholas

educating the younger people. Members who had particular skills shared their knowledge with the local children. Culturally based knowledge empowered its members by educating them in subjects that affected their daily survival as well as their spiritual and cultural well-being.

By the time Sandra was growing up in the 1950s and 1960s, her community's traditional ways of living had eroded greatly. The establishment of reservations placed restrictions on First Nations people, as did the establishment of modern education. Children were taken from their families and forced to attend distant residential schools set up by certain religious groups or were made to attend local schools run by non-Natives. The end result was the same: First Nations culture was ignored in all aspects of education and cultural awareness was lost.

For the generations of Aboriginal people who grew up in both the mainstream, non-Native world and their own community, the values of the two cultures often clashed. Traditional Maliseet values center on what people have to offer and not on what gender they happen to be; everyone plays an important role in the Maliseet community. In comparison, Western non-Native society has largely been run by men, with women being excluded from many activities and professions. It wasn't until the last century that women were given the right to vote and considered as important as or equal to men.

In 1970, when Sandra was twenty-two, she married an American non-Native and moved to

California. Her life as an airman's wife with four young children was busy, but the marriage was not to last. The couple divorced after a few years, and Sandra returned to the Tobique First Nation with her children. There she discovered that by having married a non-Native she was no longer entitled to the same housing, education, and health care opportunities as the other First Nation people of her community. Something had gone terribly wrong, and Sandra had to get to the bottom of it!

She learned that under the Canadian Indian Act, which was established in 1867 and defines who is an "Indian," she and her children had lost their status as Indians because she had married a non-Native man, but a First Nations man who marries a non-Native woman would not lose his status.

Outraged, Sandra got together with local women who were united in their belief that the Act had to be changed. They argued that the clause that stripped women of their status was a violation of their human rights. How could a government take away the essence or heritage of another human being?

In 1977, after lobbying the federal government and getting no results, Sandra went before the Human Rights Commission of the United Nations to try to abolish the clause that discriminated against First Nations women who married outside their culture. This was Sandra's chance to represent the thousands of Aboriginal women and their children who had experienced the same discrimination that she had. And she didn't stop there. Two years later, to help draw media attention to their mission, Sandra led an 82-mile (132-kilometer) protest march from Oka, Québec, to Ottawa, Ontario.

In 1981, the United Nations supported Sandra's position and found Canada had violated human rights. It took four years for the Canadian government to amend the Act and remove the controversial clause. Sandra and others like her who had lost their status were reinstated as members of their First Nations communities and were once again entitled to housing, health care, and educational benefits like other members of their bands.

In recognition of her dedication to her community and the larger First Nations communities of Canada, Sandra was awarded the Order of Canada in 1990, Canada's highest civilian honor. Two years later, she received a Governor General's Award. And in 2005, Sandra received perhaps her biggest honor. She got a call at home from Paul Martin, Canada's then prime minister. At first she didn't believe who was on the other end of the phone, but what he had to say would change her life in ways she never expected. He offered her the position of senator in the federal government.

Sandra had already been many things at different times during her life. She had been a carpenter who had built her home and her mother's home, a home care worker, an administrator, and, at the time of the prime minister's call, a woman who was between jobs and looking for her next opportunity. Never had she dreamed of being a senator, but she quickly accepted the prime minister's offer.

Sandra Lovelace Nicholas's success in changing an unfair Canadian law is an inspiring example, which proves that one woman can make a difference in correcting a national injustice. She brings cultural diversity to the Senate and provides a rare voice for First Nations people within the federal government. Her pride, strength, and determination make her an international role model for all women who continue to fight for fair treatment.

PHOTO CREDITS

Front Cover:

Susan Aglukark: Photo by Denise Grant, courtesy of Aglukark Entertainment Inc.

Pauline Johnson-Tekahionwake: Courtesy of the Brant Museum and Archives

Mary Kim Titla: Courtesy of Mary Kim Titla

Wilma Mankiller: Photo by Tom Gilbert, Chief Photographer, *Tulsa World*

Winona LaDuke: Photo by Rick Mickelson, University of Wisconsin-Eau Claire

Back Cover:

Mary Kim Titla: Courtesy of Mary Kim Titla

Pauline Johnson-Tekahionwake: Courtesy of the Brant Museum and Archives

Suzanne Rochon-Burnett: Photo by Julie Jocsak, *Osprey's Niagara Magazine*, May 2005, article by Linda Bramble

Interior:

Suzanne Rochon-Burnett: Photo by Julie Jocsak, *Osprey's Niagara Magazine*, May 2005, article by Linda Bramble

Pauline Johnson-Tekahionwake: Courtesy of the Brant Museum and Archives

Thocmetony (Sarah) Winnemucca:
   1-2 Courtesy Nevada Historical Society
   3 Mark McLaughlin/Mic Mac Publishing

Maria Tallchief: © 1978 Maurice Seymore/MPTV.net

Wilma Mankiller: Photo by Tom Gilbert, Chief Photographer, *Tulsa World*

Mary Kim Titla: Courtesy of Mary Kim Titla

Lorna B. Williams: Photo courtesy *Grizzly Bear Teachings 2006*

Susan Aglukark: Photo by Denise Grant, courtesy of Aglukark Entertainment Inc.

Winona LaDuke:

   1 Courtesy Honor the Earth

   2 Courtesy White Earth Land Recovery

   3 Photo by Rick Mickelson, University of Wisconsin-Eau Claire

Sandra Lovelace Nicholas: Courtesy Law Clerk and Parliamentary Council, Ottawa, Ontario